Debt and Poverty Freedom

WITH THE HOLY GHOST

WORKBOOK

Written by Kay Nash

Debt and Poverty Freedom with The Holy Ghost Workbook

Copyright © 2021 Kristen Nash

Kay Nash Ministries
www.KayNashMinistries.com

Scripture quotations marked (NKJV) are taken from the New King James Version®. Copyright © 1982 by Thomas Nelson. Used by permission. All rights reserved. Scripture quotations marked (NLT) are taken from the Holy Bible, New Living Translation, copyright ©1996, 2004, 2007, 2013, 2015 by Tyndale House Foundation. Used by permission of Tyndale House Publishers, Inc., Carol Stream, Illinois 60188. All rights reserved. Scripture quotations marked (ESV) are from the ESV® Bible (The Holy Bible, English Standard Version®), copyright © 2001 by Crossway, a publishing ministry of Good News Publishers. Used by permission. All rights reserved. Scripture quotations marked (NASB) are taken from the New American Standard Bible® (NASB), Copyright © 1960, 1962, 1963, 1968, 1971, 1972, 1973, 1975, 1977, 1995 by The Lockman Foundation. Used by permission. www.Lockman.org. Scripture quotations marked (BSB) are from The Holy Bible, Berean Study Bible, BSB. Copyright ©2016, 2018 by Bible Hub. Used by Permission. All Rights Reserved Worldwide.

Italics, bold, underlines and parenthesis in Scripture quotations have been added by the author for emphasis.

ISBN: 978-1-387-32942-7

Cover Design by Ryan (Timothy) Nash
Copyright © 2021

Introduction

If you are reading this workbook, it is probably because you are in debt or struggling with poverty. I get it, and I was once there too. Don't feel alone. Debt is a serious problem in the United States, where I live, and in other countries as well. Recent statistics I read said around 80% of Americans and 85% of people in the U.K. are in debt, and one survey says two in five Canadians believe "they will be in debt the rest of their lives"! What is going on with money in our world? How did we get here? Why are so many people in debt and some feeling so hopeless about it? Is income really the problem, or is it something more?

I personally believe there is way more going on than just people needing an increase in their income (though that is obviously part of it for sure). What you must understand is that there are demonic spirits that want people to be in debt! You must also know that the Bible tells us that our battle is not against flesh and blood but against principalities (Ephesians 6:12). But why would demons want us to be in debt? Quite simply, they want us in bondage to things. Think about it this way: If a demon has you stuck in mountains of debt it's harder for you to focus on your calling, as you are making decisions based only on money. As Christian believers we shouldn't be making decisions based on if we have enough money to do this or that, but rather on what the Holy Spirit is leading us to do. Before we start this journey, I want you to make a commitment right now not to make any more decisions based solely on money, but instead to do what the Lord told you to. This will be hard when you first start, as you will have to battle your mind, but you cannot let money control you. We cannot give into mammon as the Bible warns:

"No one can serve two masters; for either he will hate the one and love the other, or else he will be loyal to the one and despise the other. You cannot serve God and mammon."
Matthew 6:24 (NKJV)

I have personally witnessed what it's like when you don't let money control all your decisions. It's amazing! Often God gives you more money when you submit to His will, because He can trust you. When you make decisions based on paying bills or survival, money can easily become an idol. Wanting to pay bills is not wrong, but it is the heart posture that matters. Would you do what God said with the money even if it didn't make sense in the natural? Living a lifestyle of radical financial obedience by obeying the Holy Ghost, and trying to survive by letting money lead your decisions are two very different lifestyles.

As a minister of the Lord, I have traveled to different countries and states and have seen firsthand the hardships God's people face financially. It is very sad for many, and I feel your pain. I have been there. Often in my travels God has had me do altar calls for people wanting to be debt free or create wealth in their lives, and close to the entire room will come up to the altar. I was shocked the first time it happened, but now I am used to it, as it is a spiritual pandemic in the body of Christ, one that people everywhere need to be set free from.

God's people are struggling with money in masses, but I believe there is a way out. It will take incorporating spiritual, biblical and practical principles. It will take work, but I believe any believer can do this. I did this personally; this is not a concept I read in a book but something the Lord taught me through His Word and Spirit. These principles transformed my life from being $22,000 in debt and growing up mostly in poverty, to being fully debt free and not having to work for anyone besides the Lord, having my full dependence on Him. Notice I didn't say I was financially independent; I am not. If it was not for the blessing of God, I would still be in bondage. But His loving kindness showed me a way out, a better way, and I want to show that to you. Some things in this workbook may challenge you, so feel free to go to the Lord about them if they do. But I want to encourage you that there is another side. I have seen it and have a heart for all God's people to be financially free so they can do whatever He wants them to, and so that His will may come about on the Earth.

I am going to start this workbook by telling you my full financial story in hopes you can understand where I came from compared to where I am now. Then we will go into practical tips and exercises to set you free. Are you ready to be debt and poverty free? Let's go, more is waiting!

Part 1

From Bondage to Abundance - My Financial Journey

I grew up relatively poor in New York. We were still able to buy food, have clothes and have a place to live though, so in some ways we were blessed. My mother was also able to stay home with one of my sisters and I. Things were generally humble but they were fine in that season, but they would soon change. My Dad was diagnosed with a disease called Ehlers-Danlos Syndrome, which is a rare disease that only affects 200,000 Americans per year. People with this disease have a median life expectancy of 40-48 years old, and my dad sadly succumbed to that statistic. I watched as my Dad slowly became very skinny and eventually died at 42 years old.

My dad knew it was coming, as the Lord warned him shortly before he died and told him his time was coming. My dad said to the Lord He would leave but asked the Lord to take care of his girls, and though it has been tough at times I can truly say the Lord takes care of me.

Soon after the encounter my father's heart stopped, and he died. We received a small pension and monthly allowance from my father's job, but it wasn't a lot. My mom tried to work different jobs to keep up with the bills, but it wasn't enough.

One night while it was dark, I was outside our home and I saw a man come and get in our car and start driving it away. I quickly told my mom there was a "thief", and I started running down the road after the "thief". But my mom told me to come back inside and to let him take the car. She explained to me that it was being repossessed, which meant the bills weren't paid on time and it could be taken away. She would also soon tell me that we were going through a bankruptcy and would lose our house as well. I watched my mom try to sell off our stove, dishwasher, anything to get some cash before they locked up the doors to our house. This experience was horrifying for me being such a young age (maybe eight or nine), but I knew even then that I had to start figuring out ways to make money so we could survive and live differently.

I started working as a babysitter around 10 years old, then at 14 I worked at a plant nursery, and around 16 I worked at a pizza place, a shoe store and at Kmart. With these jobs I was able to give and lend money to my mom, and was able to buy conditioner, something my mom had said was a waste of money at the time. But with my frizzy hair this was much desired by me, and I was able to get it through these little jobs I did. This taught me a principle early on: work can produce desired results.

I then got deeper into the food industry by becoming a waitress and eventually a restaurant manager, and I was starting to make pretty decent money for a young person, and it felt good. But then I made two huge financial mistakes. Had I known the word of God and the Holy Spirit, maybe I wouldn't have. So let me save you some time by learning from my experiences.

My First Debt
(Student Loan)

The first mistake was taking out a student loan "just in case I needed one". I was advised by some people close to me that this would be the right decision... Wrong! This was a huge mistake that I would regret later. You see, I had full scholarships that covered my college tuition and also some grants that gave me partial room and board. But there were some things that it didn't cover, such as bills, food, gas and summer expenses. But I couldn't believe God back then for those simple things, as I had yet to learn how to believe Him for money. At the time I believed things had to "make sense" to move forward.

So, I took out a student loan. At first it didn't seem to affect me much, as I didn't have to pay it off until I got out of college, so I didn't think it was a big deal. However, six months after college the companies came straight for me with large monthly payments. It was fun to have extra money in college, but I truly paid the cost later. If I knew then what I do now, I would never have taken out that loan! I didn't understand trusting the Lord as my provider. When you really trust the Lord with all your soul, debt is no longer necessary, as He provides for what He calls for you to do.

My Second Debt
(Car Loan)

The second unsmart financial mistake I made was taking collision coverage off my car insurance when I had a fully paid off car. I know, not my brightest moment, but I was trying to cut my monthly expenses as I wasn't making a lot each month in that season. I had worked hard in college to buy a brand new car. In one year, I had put about half the money down and then paid off the other half by the end of that same year. Six months after I took collision coverage off my car; I got into an accident on a rainy night, totaling my car to the point where it was undriveable, and my basic insurance refused to cover any of it.

So now I had large student loan payments each month, no car, and wasn't making much in pay. Basically, I was just trying to get by. At the time I was working my first television job, and was only making $13,000 a year (they pay you awfully in Television in the beginning because so many people want the job it is considered a "privilege" to work in the industry, at least that's what they say). This was a hard time for me, and I was drowning financially. But in time things would change, and I started moving up the corporate ladder in Television. I started to make double and triple my salary as I climbed to new positions. Soon I decided it was time to get a reliable car again, as the clunker cars I was buying just kept breaking down and I needed a reliable car to get to work.

So I decided what I would do is take out a brand new car loan with no money down. Yes I know, not a good idea. However, in Television what you drove seemed to matter. A lot of outwardly things are emphasized in that industry. So I made this decision not only to get a reliable car, but I wanted something nice enough that I wouldn't be embarrassed around co-workers. If I am honest, I felt no peace when I signed the paperwork, but I didn't know the Holy Spirit as well as I do now. So I took out the loan and now had a large car payment and a large student loan payment each month. You think this would be bad enough, but the third debt was on its way...

My Third Debt
(Hospital Bills)

The next debt came while I was in ministry school. Shortly after I took out that car loan, the Lord asked me to quit my job and just follow Him blindly. So, I listened and trusted. But soon He would continue His instructions, and soon I would be moving out of the state with no job and starting to rack up debt. I moved to a state where I knew no one and would ultimately end up attending a small ministry school there. While there one night, I became very ill, and it became so bad that I felt like I just couldn't go on. As a person who believes in supernatural physical healing, I did everything I could to pray away this feeling, but I felt the Lord tell me, "Go to the hospital and I will pay for it." So I did, and it turned out that I was completely dehydrated of fluids, and they had to pump me full of liquids to keep me alive. Thankfully I was fine after that, but it came with a hefty bill and now I was in three different debts. It was getting overwhelming, and I had no job.

My Fourth Debt
(Credit Cards)

Shortly after this, I moved back to Florida where I would end up starting my own ministry. I didn't know that at the time, I just listened when God said to move back. But when He did call me to my own ministry, it was hard financially. The area didn't really understand the prophetic, nor did they understand the importance of giving into prophetic ministries. I also had a hard time ever asking for money, not wanting to appear as needy or commercializing the gospel. But God healed me from this in time, as the Bible says a worker is worthy of his wages (1 Timothy 5:18), and God convinced me that I deserved to eat healthy food and be taken care of as His daughter. But that took time for me to understand. I also didn't understand the Blessing of the Lord (Proverbs 10:22) and how it operates, so we were broke in the early years of ministry. It was so bad that we were even putting groceries on credit cards, which would accumulate my fourth kind of debt. I felt like I was drowning financially, but I kept on preaching, and people were getting physically healed, hearing God and beginning to prophesy. Revival was happening in our area, but my bank account was drained.

I had accumulated $22,000 in debt. I was frustrated and overwhelmed. I was a tither and serving the Lord, so why did I struggle so much financially? I would soon realize there were many principles of wealth I needed to learn from God's word. Hidden, but accessible to all.

With the mass amount of debt I had, I decided one day that I would not accumulate anymore, as I couldn't let that number get any bigger. So I cut up all my credit cards and refused to use them anymore. This was scary, but I wanted God to show up and meet my needs rather than just charging away and going into more financial bondage.

Another breaking point I had that forced me to change was when my husband Ryan and I were so broke that for one whole week we literally had to pick up change off the ground to buy ramen packets to survive. After several days of only eating ramen, we both felt awful physically, and I knew this wasn't how God wanted us to live. How could this be an abundant life promised in John 10:10? We couldn't go out with friends, we couldn't eat healthily, and we couldn't buy personal products to make us feel good (such as vitamins, etc...). The anxiety I felt in this season around money was so high. I was talking to Ryan about it all the time. I decided it was time to learn about money from God's word, and to start taking up donations in the ministry. When I first started asking for money after years of not asking for it, some people were offended, as they wanted to just milk me until I was dry.

Others said they had always wondered how to give into my ministry but didn't know how. The reactions I got were split, and it was scary, but the Bible says:

"...Thou shalt not muzzle the ox that treadeth out the corn. and, the labourer is worthy of his reward."
1 Timothy 5:8 (KJV)

I wasn't the best at taking up donations in the beginning, sometimes I would, and other times I would get scared and not ask. So I also started making and selling products to supplement our income. This started to turn things around slowly and really was a time of learning for me about Godly finances. I really began to understand my value as a child of God financially through scripture. I also believe that working hard on projects the Lord gave me, gaining a Godly understanding of the current financial culture, and the Holy Spirit's personal advice for me became a fire that changed my life.

Getting Out of Debt

My first debt that I paid off was the hospital bill I talked about earlier, and most of it was paid off supernaturally. Like I said earlier, God told me He would pay for the hospital visit, but it wasn't right away. It was probably another four months before that would come about. So I paid the minimum payments for the first four months of about $30 or so.

Then I received a prophetic word from one of the women's pastors at my church when I was talking to her about the hospital bill being a weight on me. She told me to inquire of the hospital to see if they had a charity that paid off bills. I inquired and they did! I just had to fill out an application. On the application it asked, "Why can you not pay this bill?" and I said, "I am in ministry school". That's all I said, and you know what? It was approved and they canceled my hospital bill! God had paid the bill just like that. I had to submit to authority and His prophetic word over my life, but that was all. I was honest, I didn't make up a sad tale playing the victim, I just put what I felt in my heart and I was free. Simple obedience brings many results. In the Bible it says:

> *"...Hear me, Judah and inhabitants of Jerusalem! Believe in*
> *the LORD your God, and you will be established;*
> *believe his prophets, and you will succeed."*
> *2 Chronicles 20:20 (ESV)*

I believed my prophetic pastor and listened to what she said, I told the truth and acted on what God told me through her, and thousands of dollars in debt was gone! You can have the same results as me. Listen to prophets, be honest and do what God told you to do, and He can cancel debts! He is Yah!

The next big one was my student loan. This one took sacrifice, and God did not do it in the same way. I think it is interesting how I went through different processes for each debt as it is not a formula to get out of debt in the Spirit but rather obedience to the Holy Ghost and His Word that matters, as well as having a right heart before Him.

God told me to start putting $500 a month toward the loan. At the time, I was only making about $26,000 a year so it was a big sacrifice. I was living alone (this was before I was married) and this left me $35 a week for food. At the time I was gluten free, and for those of you who have lived like this, you know gluten free foods can be rather expensive. But I did it anyway. Basically, I bought eggs and gluten free waffles for breakfast, chicken salad for lunch and chicken and rice for dinner, and I ate that every day. I didn't even have salt or pepper in my house, I lived so simply. I remember a girlfriend coming over my house and being like, "Where is all your food? Why do you not have salt and pepper?" I told her what I was doing, and she felt bad and went and bought me salt and pepper. It was hard living this way, but I did this for five months and was able to pay off $2,500 of my student loans. I am glad I sacrificed and listened to God's advice so it wasn't a huge burden for me later on, and I could focus on God and what He was saying, not on paying student loan debt.

In the Bible it says:

"For the drunkard and the glutton will come to poverty,
and drowsiness will clothe them in rags."
Proverbs 23:21 (BSB)

If you cannot control your food intake, this can waste a lot of money. I basically went without desserts or any extras for a long time. But because of this and listening to the Word of the Lord, I was able to get out of my student loan debt quicker than most. See where you can cut back on food, as the Lord leads. I believe health is important and would have not done this if the Lord had not told me to as I realize eating the same thing every day is not the best, but I knew He would sustain me. Be healthy but save where you can when you are getting out of debt. Even ask God for a food plan if possible. He will put things on sale sometimes if He told you to buy them, and He knows what your body needs.

The next thing I decided to conquer was my credit cards. I made a list of my smallest card amounts to my largest, and started tackling the smallest ones first. By this time Ryan and I were married. The first thing I did was start couponing. Now, I do believe couponing can become an idol, because you can spend an hour looking for a $1 coupon, which means you paid yourself $1 for that hour.. So you have to be cautious of this and not become obsessed, but use wisdom from the Lord and you can get some serious deals with coupons. Make a list of things you buy every week and then go see if you can find coupons for those things online. You might be surprised by what is out there. Also, a girlfriend told me this tip: you can sometimes use two coupons on the same product. You can use a manufacturer's coupon (from the brand that produces the product), and a store coupon (say a Publix or Walmart coupon) and "stack" them. This provides large savings and sometimes free stuff.

I also started doing surveys online. This doesn't make a lot of money, but if you have a small credit card (say, $300 - $500), these little things can add up and help you pay it off quickly. It doesn't have to be these things, but see if there are small things you can do to conquer your smaller debts. The Bible says:

"Catch all the foxes, those little foxes, before they ruin the vineyard of love, for the grapevines are blossoming!"
Song of Solomon 2:15 (NLT)

Sometimes it is the little things we are not doing that can stop us from getting big breakthroughs. Ask God if there are any small things you can do to get extra money. You may be surprised at what He shows you!!

I also sold things. You would be amazed at the amount of junk the average person has that they don't need. Some things were hard to part with, but when you see the results it is worth it. You can sell on eBay, which my husband and I did. Ryan is a good photographer, so he was able to take good pictures. Ryan and I had a lot of random electronics, movies, games, etc. that we didn't need (plus some movies were demonic and we didn't need them spiritually or physically). You can also do this at pawn shops. Don't pawn your stuff, but just sell it flat out and get the cash and put it towards your debt. Do you have an old VCR? DVD player? Movies? CDs that you shouldn't be listening to, or an old phone, etc.? Technology often makes some quick money. I also sold purses, clothes and wallets on luxury resale websites and started making small checks off of that. If you have any designer or mid-range designer items, sell them if you don't use them and put that towards your debt. Obviously do all these things as the Lord leads because it is His prompting that brings the most profit.

It was the small things that got us out of credit card debt. It may be a large thing for you, but either way, ask the Lord. The Bible says:

"The LORD your God will drive out these nations before you little by little. You will not be enabled to eliminate them all at once, or the wild animals would multiply around you."
Deuteronomy 7:22 (BSB)

Sometimes debt freedom doesn't come overnight. It may come little by little, and that is okay. Sometimes this is part of the process. God doesn't enable you. Sometimes He blesses, but not enables. He often lets you feel the process and learn from it, so you don't get into debt again. Honestly having less stuff was very freeing and it helped us focus more on the call of God in our lives in that season. Clutter can cause confusion and waste time. Even if you don't sell your items and give them to charity or something, eliminating unnecessary stuff can lead to clarity in knowing what you need to do next in breaking poverty and getting debt free.

The last thing was my car loan. I cannot even begin to describe to you the demonic nature behind this debt. This is when I started realizing that there was more to debt freedom than just discipline and money management. Sometimes there is a demon you are battling, as the company you owe the debt to can be ruled by a principality. The car company I owed money to kept changing debt collectors. As I would start to make progress in paying off the car debt, my debt would be sold off to another debt collector. These people were rude and pushy. There were also month long gaps between these company switches, and they would charge me interest for "not paying" even though there was no way I could pay them during that time. They either didn't have an online platform to pay on, or they would not provide me information on how to pay until they slapped on late fees and interest charges. It was so bizarre, as I had bought this car brand new from the dealership, not some sketchy place. But what you see on the outside is not always what is on the inside. I kept thinking I owed a certain amount, and then I would owe more. It felt like this was a game to them and I just couldn't get out of it. I would pray about this often, not understanding what to do.

Then one day the Lord spoke to me and told me to break the principality over the company. Within a short period of time, the debt was sold again and this time I got a great company managing the debt, and got on a first name basis with one of the collectors. They knew when I called and would take any payment whenever I wanted over the phone. So every time I had extra money, I sent it to them. Then one morning the Lord spoke to me and told me to call them that same day and offer a certain amount to pay off the rest of the debt, which was half of what I owed. They counter offered $100 more, so I paid it off that day and got half off the debt, just like that. Oh my friends, the Word of the Lord! Prayer is so important. I also believe it was important that I built a relationship with the company and was nice to them. I have heard before that you should yell and scream at debt collectors. I disagree. These are people, and when these people feel like you respect them, they are more likely to work with you. Now you shouldn't do this out of manipulation (being nice to get something). I had no idea the Lord was going to tell me one morning to offer half of what I owed. You should be nice because we are representatives of Christ.

Now I was free of all my debt. I was free of bondage. I honestly felt lighter after this. I think there were principalities holding me back, and when they were gone my money changed. The Bible says:

"The rich rule over the poor, and the
borrower is slave to the lender."
Proverbs 22:7 (BSB)

When you get free of debt, your slavery ceases and you are free. The Bible encourages us to get free from slavery, even if were that way when Christ called us.

"Were you a slave when you were called?
Do not let it concern you—but if you can gain
your freedom, take the opportunity."
1 Corinthians 7:21 (BSB)

We are supposed to gain our freedom if possible, so we can follow Christ however He wants us to and not be controlled by demons, companies or money.

Building Wealth

Less than three hours after getting out of debt, I received a phone call that I would be receiving a $10,000 check to buy a new car. What I didn't tell you before is that the car I was in debt over had been repossessed, so I was paying a company for something I didn't even have anymore, and this went on for years. Many people wouldn't do this, they would say, "Well I don't own that car anymore, so I am not paying for it!" However, you signed a contract, and you have to pay what you owe. I believe God honored me for paying them off even though I had nothing to show for it by giving me a free car afterwards. The person that gave the money had no idea that I had paid off an old car loan that day. They were just doing what they felt to do that day.

But God knew. Even as I write this years later, it seems surreal that I signed for a car and went into tons of debt for it, and it was taken away. Then in one phone call God just gave me a car, paid for in cash with no strings attached. My friends, wait on the Lord and do His will. There are many miracles for you as you walk this journey of debt and poverty freedom. It won't always be easy, but it is worth it. You owe it to yourself to be free of poverty and debt. In this place we find more freedom in Christ and more peace.

After this I was debt free and had a paid off car, but I still had to learn to save money. The Bible says:

> *"The wise have wealth and luxury,*
> *but fools spend whatever they get."*
> *Proverbs 21:20 (NLT)*

I had to decide not to be a fool and spend every dollar that came through my hands but rather learn to save for things the Lord wanted me to. I was also starting to focus on expanding His kingdom and building a legacy.

*"A good man leaves an inheritance to his children's children,
but the sinner's wealth is passed to the righteous."*
Proverbs 13:22 (BSB)

This was a hard process, as when you finally get money that doesn't have to go to bills or basic needs you want to buy stuff. But if you delay gratification, you can buy better stuff you want later.

Another important thing in wealth building is the "Blessing of the Lord". It was about year after getting out of debt that the Blessing of the Lord came on my life. I personally believe the Lord blessing you is one of the biggest factors to wealth that there is.

*"The blessing of the LORD makes one rich,
and He adds no sorrow with it."*
Proverbs 10:22 (NKJV)

Ask the Lord for His blessing if you are trying to build wealth and things will change for you if He gives it. Keep interceding until it comes. I used to walk around just saying "I have the Blessing of the Lord", as that is what I was taught. But nothing in my life changed. You know why? Because God didn't give it to me. You can claim you are blessed every day, but only God can give the Blessing of the Lord. Think about in the Bible when a parent blesses a son. The son doesn't just go around claiming he is blessed; no, the father actually speaks forth the blessing on him. The same is true with God, He has to decide to bless you in order for the blessing to operate. One day the blessing appeared in prayer. I felt a tangible presence on my hands and asked the Lord what it was, and He said "It is the Blessing of the Lord." My life almost instantly changed financially. I can't even describe it fully, it was supernatural. Within months my husband was able to quit his job after years of wanting to leave, and work for the ministry full time. The Blessing of the Lord made the way. Then I had to start saving what came in.

It was hard for me to save money just for the sake of saving it. It seemed wrong or greedy to me. However, when I started saving money for specific goals, I was successful. If you've been having a problem saving money and don't have exact goals, this may be why. Ask the Lord for His savings goals for you and you will see Him show up, because when you ask Him, He then has already anointed the money to come in. You just have to do what He says.

Though this whole story is only a few pages long in this book, these changes didn't happen overnight. It took a lot of prayer, education, obedience and discipline to become debt and poverty free. It will take time, as you have to unlearn things and relearn them with Christ. His Word is powerful, and as you study it you will be surprised at how much it tells you about money. If applied to your life, things will change drastically.

Part 2

Poverty Free - Biblical Proverbs To Break Poverty

If you want to break debt and build wealth for real and not play games with this, you need to take what I am going to say in this chapter seriously. You can read this as head knowledge, but if you apply this to your life you will become poverty free. Solomon was the richest man in the world during his time and he wrote a lot of the principles I am going to mention. If you can apply them, you can be poverty free.

Don't Give In To Gluttony

"For the drunkard and the glutton shall come to poverty: and drowsiness shall clothe a man with rags."
Proverbs 23:21 (KJV)

This is a hard one because weight or body shape doesn't necessarily mean you are a glutton. So we can't assume someone is a glutton by the outwardly, but rather it is something you and the Lord must discuss to really know your heart.

Now why does the Bible say being a glutton will bring you to poverty? Why is that true? There are several factors I want you to consider. The first is that if you buy too much food, then you are spending more money than you should be. This money could go to paying off debt or purchasing something else you desire. It quickly adds up and you end up wondering "Where has my money gone?" It is in your belly only to be digested and exited. You have nothing to show for it after that. It's one thing if you are spending your money on foods for health, it is another thing to gorge yourself to feel numb and avoid pain. I have heard it said before that for many poor, one of their main luxuries is food. It is often their reward or their comfort, and I think there are times to eat a great meal and to enjoy yourself. Your birthday, a wedding, etc. But if that is all the time, you may be giving into gluttony.

Giving into gluttony can be a temptation to avoid issues. Remember, the Bible says out of the heart flow the issues of life (Proverbs 4:23). When you deal with pain or a bad day by eating bad food, your heart's issues still are there and you have solved nothing. For a moment you feel better, but soon the issue will arise again. Then you eat again, and an addictive cycle can be produced. This must be broken through Christ and prayer. Instead, when you want to eat to deal with emotional pain, get before the Lord, journal, and tell Him how you are feeling. Then see if He will speak to you. His word will heal.

The second reason gluttony can lead to poverty is being "food drunk". You know what I am talking about, when you eat so much food that you need to take a significant break after eating to digest, and you feel sluggish. One day the Lord spoke to me and said, "You need to identify if the food you are eating is 'fuel or drool.'" In other words, is this food going to give you energy to get things done, or is it going to make you pass out on the couch and not be able to move. This lack of motion can cause poverty over time, as you may spend time every night "recovering" from what you ate, when you could be working your land.

The third reason gluttony can lead to poverty is health issues. When you have health issues from bad foods going into your body, it is going to slow you down in moving toward your destiny. It will also cost you money in medication to treat the issues, and money in doctor visits.

You can help avoid all of these issues by choosing to ask the Lord what to eat for each meal. Even make a Holy Spirit guided grocery list. This can be hard at times as your body or a demon may be encouraging you to eat something else, but the Lord is not rigid. He still lets me eat cookies and things I like, but in moderation.

This can also be a big safety measure, as when you eat foods the Lord wants you to and avoid the other ones, you may stop yourself from getting food poisoning. If He says no to certain food, just trust. If He is trying to get you to eat something, know that your body needs it.

Don't Be Addicted To Oil

"He who loves pleasure will become poor;
the one who loves wine and oil will never be rich."
Proverbs 21:17 (BSB)

We are going to use this verse several times, as you can see there is more to it, but for this section we are going to talk about oil. This is a hard principle to understand, but the Bible says that loving oil will cause one to never be rich. How can this be and why does this matter?

Oil can be very expensive. When you get into certain oils from certain locations the price can be very high. Some people collect oils and indulge in them like wine. You must remember, these are consumable items. Once you use them they are gone, and the money you spent on them is gone too. That's money you could have invested in things that would make you more money, but instead it is poured on your plate. It is not wrong to indulge every once in a while, but to indulge consistently is a problem.

Another way that I currently see oil being used as an addiction is in the area of essential oils. I see women with many different pricey essential oils, and each one is supposed to do a different thing, apparently 'curing' certain issues. But a cure means something is done, treatment is ongoing. So you have to keep buying it and the company gets richer and richer. There is often a spirit of witchcraft here (which is often a controlling spirit) and can become financial pitfall that never ends. One of the ways a spirit witchcraft works is it causes you to be addicted to something that never provides a real solution. People who operate in witchcraft don't care about you, but rather are trying to build something for themselves. These companies profit off of sick women and give them temporary relief from a problem (if any), when these ladies really need a blast from the Holy Ghost and to cast out a spirit of infirmity or whatever demon is ailing them.

Once at a conference I was speaking at, there was a woman looking for an essential oils booth to get healing from feeling sick. God was about to set this woman up. I just happened to be back in that area, and the person with the oil booth had gone on break. I asked the woman what she was doing back there, and she said she wanted some oil so she could be well. I said, "Woman, all you need is anointing oil." I anointed her and she fell out in the spirit by the product tables and was healed from her sickness. There is only one oil you need: oil that carries the anointing of God! Honestly you don't need oil to be healed (though it can help if it was prayed over), but the presence of God and the Blood of Jesus is all you need.

There are also cosmetic oils as well. To be clear, buying oil isn't bad, it is the addiction to it that is a problem, as it will be a financial drain over time.

Ask the Lord what oils to buy and not to buy, but don't get addicted.

Don't Give In To Fear

*"The rich man's goods are his strong city: but the
fear of the needy is their poverty."*
Proverbs 10:15 (GNV)

When God highlighted this verse to me for the first time, I was stunned that I had never heard anyone talk about it before. This verse basically tells us that fear causes poverty, and that when needy people walk in fear, they become poor. What a shocking, eye opening verse. We have been told for too long "do it afraid." No my friends, fear is a demon. We don't do things afraid, we cast out a spirit of fear and walk in authority and power as we are powerful beings made by God. We should not be put into shaking by the devil.

So practically speaking, how can fear lead to poverty? Think about it this way: maybe God tells you to apply for a certain job, but the devil convinces you out of fear that the job is beyond you and makes you feel like you could not be all it wants you to be. So then you don't apply for the job, and now you are poor. We must be obedient to the Lord if we want true financial success, as fear leads to poverty. Fear and the Holy Spirit are conflicting spirits. The Holy Spirit wants you to grow and be fruitful and multiply; fear wants you to be small and stay where you are. Choose right now not to let fear stop you from doing the Lord's will in your life. The next time you feel fear say, "I rebuke the spirit of fear in Jesus name!" or whatever the Lord prompts you to say, and get that demon out of there! Your provision is on the other side!

> *"For God has not given us a spirit of fear,*
> *but of power and of love and of a sound mind."*
> *2 Timothy 1:7(NKJV)*

Fear is not of God as it pulls back. Faith leaps ahead. Now I will say that faith also listens to God. You don't want to just be doing things "in faith" that God has not anointed, as it could lead to a lack of results. But the righteous walk by faith (2 Corinthians 5:7).

Let go of fear today if He is calling you to do something.

Harlotry Can Cause Poverty

> *"For a prostitute will bring you to poverty, but sleeping*
> *with another man's wife will cost you your life."*
> *Proverbs 6:26 (NLT)*

When you commit harlotry or any sexual perversion (masturbation, watching pornography, being with a prostitute, having sex before marriage, etc.), your finances can get messed up.

First, you waste time committing the act, which could be used for working your land. Then you waste more time feeling ashamed by the acts. Then you may catch a disease from the act, which will cost you time, money and your dignity.

In addition to possibly experiencing poverty financially, you may also experience it in your relationships as a result of sexual sin. When you fantasize about someone who is not your spouse, you can enter into a soul tie with them, which will make it more difficult for you to form real relationships and can also enter you into bondage with a demon. Demons project lustful images to your brain to make you touch yourself to them. Sometimes they will even touch your private parts to make you feel aroused. When you give into this, you are giving into a demon and then over time you develop a tie with this demon, and it will keep coming back. The Bible calls this "the spirit of harlotry" (Hosea 5:4). When you give into this demon, it will steal your money or more.

You may not like what I am telling you here, and some of you may be upset and tempted to stop reading this book. But do you want the truth, or do you want the nice "christian" blanket we give people? It is the truth that sets free, and if you really want out of poverty you must eradicate sexual sin from your life. You may say to me, "Well how come evil men or women with wealth have affairs and are still rich?" You must understand that they are controlled by a different kingdom. The rules of God's kingdom keep us safe and help us create wealth and prosperity if we follow them.

Too Much Wine Or Drinking Can Lead To Poverty

"Whoever loves pleasure will be a poor man;
he who loves wine and oil will not be rich."
Proverbs 21:17 (ESV)

"for the drunkard and the glutton will come to poverty..."
Proverbs 23:21 (ESV)

This is a hard one to gauge in the church, as there is no set number of drinks the Bible says is too much. We know that drinking wine is not a sin for everyone, as Jesus turned water into wine, and He would not make something for people to do that was sinful. He is perfect. However, some people can drink, and some should not. This is really an individual thing between you and the Holy Ghost. You should know if it is right or wrong for you based on what the Lord tells you individually. However, drinking too much can lead to poverty.

Alcohol costs money. I have seen friends of mine, when I was in college, spend $70 on alcohol in one night just for themselves. Others would get drunk and buy a round of shots for the bar, and then wonder why they had no money. These things add up. Sometimes a glass of wine can cost $13 or even more. If you have a couple of those a week you are really hurting your budget. If you want to get out of poverty and struggle with drinking, or just want to cut something out of your budget, cut out drinking. You don't have to be legalistic unless the Lord tells you to, but it will save you money to cut out alcohol.

Also, drinking takes up a lot of time, and you waste time being drunk and then hungover and not feeling well, etc. That's all time that you could use to work towards your future dreams and goals. You can also hurt relationships that could be profitable. No person wants to do business with a drunk; they cannot trust the erratic behavior. Over-drinkers often tend to break or destroy things in their drunkenness, which also costs money to replace or repair. You can also develop health problems from drinking too much alcohol. Some of these are high blood pressure, heart disease, stroke, liver disease, digestive problems, cancer of the breast, mouth, throat, esophagus, liver, and colon. All of these take time and money to treat. Now I am not saying one glass of wine is going to cause all these things, but abusive alcohol behavior can lead to this. Take time with the Holy Spirit to see if you should limit or stop your alcoholic intake for health, financial or even social reasons.

Sleeping Can Cause Poverty

"Love not sleep, lest thou come to poverty; open thine eyes,
and thou shalt be satisfied with bread."
Proverbs 20:13 (KJV)

Sleeping addiction is a real thing and can lead to a lack of wealth. I dealt with this a lot in college, I would just avoid issues coming up in my life by sleeping away hours of my day. But you know what? When I woke up the problem was still there. As I got more spiritually aware I realized a demon can cause this. It will come in and put you into something like a sleeping coma, and you will not wake up refreshed but rather confused how you slept so long or why. It will sometimes come with nightmares as well. I also have been on the other side of not getting enough sleep and this can be demonic as well. The devil wants you to make decisions without being in your right mind so that you make the wrong ones. Sleep is a very important thing to master for wealth.

So how can you avoid going into a demonic sleep or oversleeping? Two things (and maybe more, ask the Lord..):

1. Ask the Lord to tell you how many hours you should sleep each night, and then set an alarm for that number of hours from the time you fall asleep. Or make sure you get to bed with that many hours left before you need to wake up. If the devil is causing you to undersleep with nightmares; try playing worship music, having bibles in the room or anointing the area. If you are awakened by a demon, try your best to get back to bed.

2. Ask the Lord to wake you up when He wants you up. I hate alarms and electronics in my room at night, so this tends to work for me. I will just feel the Holy Spirit come in the room and know it is time to get up. This is not the only way, but just a thought.

When we oversleep we are wasting time and money. But undersleep can have the same effect, as we are sluggish and not alert. So our sleep is very important when it comes to getting out of poverty. We must get the right amount of sleep for us, and not compare our sleep needs to others. For me I need 7 hours to be functional, 8 hours to be well and when I am taking a day off I would say 9 hours makes me refreshed. Obviously if you are sick or haven't slept correctly in days that could be an exception to the rule.

I once slept 15 hours straight, shocking my husband. I had just gotten back from ministering in Kenya at a Pastors and Leaders conference, and wasn't sleeping much on the trip. I also didn't really get enough food or water while I was there. When I arrived home, I went straight to bed. 15 hours later, my husband started getting concerned as I am normally an undersleeper. All the years we had been together he had never seen me do anything like that, so he woke me up to make sure I was alive. My body needed that sleep. So if you need it, do it. But, if you are sleeping 15 hours every single day, there is a problem.

Oversleeping is a waste of time, and if it's not demonically induced, then it is often a sign of a deeper issue: avoidance. There is probably something you don't want to do or deal with. Lurking depression or a lack of motivation can also be factors in oversleeping, and I get that. There have been days where I just don't want to get up. But if you give in to that too often, it's probably a reason why you may be poor. This is a poverty cycle. I don't want to get up because I am poor and have nothing to live for, so I will sleep away my life, but then I remain poor. Instead, you need to have an identity shift, knowing you are an heir of Christ and you are not poor, as your father Yah owns the entire world. As you work the land the Lord has given you He will bless you. When you first tell yourself you are not poor, you may feel like a liar or delusional. However, over time of telling yourself 'you are wealthy', and doing what you feel the Lord directing you to do, you will most likely become rich. The Lord rewards those who work for Him. Get up, work your land and become prosperous.

Beware Of Too Much Pleasure

"Whoever loves pleasure (pastime) will be a poor man;
he who loves wine and oil will not be rich."
Proverbs 21:17 (ESV)

Here are some things that will make you poor: Too much TV watching, too much game playing, too much vacationing (this is a bad one we will get into in a second), too much sports watching, too much anything that is not working your land can be bad. These things can be good for workaholics or when you need a rest, but too much of these things is bad. Try this: live your week or month normally and write down how much time you spend each day doing extracurricular activities. Then ask yourself and the Lord whether that is too much. I am not saying don't have fun but do it in smaller doses as we should not love it so much that we don't work.

My husband and I recently went to West Palm Beach for Valentine's Day weekend as our babymoon before our first child. It was a two day trip, but it was paid for by hotel points. So in other words I paid no money for the room we stayed in, and since it was still in Florida we just drove there. So the trip cost us gas and food, but just two days was enough to have a good time with my husband.

I have found the art of not paying for many of my vacations by using reward programs. When you're loyal to certain companies they will reward you with points. However, we still don't currently vacation very often. Maybe once or twice a year we go somewhere for one or two days, but for many years when we were paying off debt we didn't go anywhere. Vacations are expensive and often unnecessary, especially if you are poor or paying off debt. I have even seen people pay for a vacation on a credit card saying, "we need this, we will pay it off later." No, you obviously need to work if you can't afford it.

What do you really need a vacation from anyway? Why is being with your family at home not good enough for most of the time? Because my husband and I work from home, our home is also our office. So we need to get away every once in a while to feel like we don't live at work. But if you work outside of the home, shouldn't your home be a relaxing environment? If it is not, there may be something deeper there. What are you running from? Also, the alcohol and gluttony issue can become more of a temptation when you're on a vacation. My husband and I often fast a meal on a vacation if we know we are going to go out for a large meal that night. This saves money and helps us not feel so bloated and sluggish.

TV can also be an issue. Wine or ice cream can often pair with television, and you can end up sitting there for hours watching others move ahead in their lives, getting paid for you to watch them while you are sluggish and wasting time. Try giving yourself a time limit or a "number of shows" limit per day, or cut it out completely if the Lord wills you to. This will help you have more time to make money. Track your television consumption and you may be shocked to realize all the time you are wasting, not to mention that most of it is trash and can make your mind feel cluttered or let in demons. Watch what the Lord has approved you to, and for the amount of time you and Him feel comfortable with.

Other issues could be attending too many sporting events or maybe a poker league, or going out to eat with girlfriends too often, etc. Whatever it is, ask the Lord if there is too much pastime in your life and what you should replace it with for your destiny.

Don't Babble

"In all labor there is profit, but idle chatter leads only to poverty."
Proverbs 14:23 (NKJV)

Talking too much about nothing can lead to poverty. I think we all need to vent sometimes, but if you are just babbling, often this can stop you from achieving your goals and working your lane for Christ.

Sometimes I just want to shake people when they are going on and on about seemingly nothing and be like "what are you talking about?" The truth is some people just like to hear themselves talk and ramble on about nothing. If you are going to talk to someone, don't waste their time or yours by rambling. They may get annoyed and pull away from you, which could lead to poverty. Think about it this way, if you are hanging around a bunch of rich people and start rambling, they are probably going to avoid you. The truth is rich people are often busy and want people who just get to the point. You could have made a deal with them, but instead you wasted their time and yours. Plus talking about dreams versus doing the dreams are two very different things. Go and do the dreams.

I will never forget this season of life in my twenties when I was part of a group of young adults who would just talk all night long, all the time. Sometimes it could be 4 or 5am before these groups would stop. People would be talking about God, money, conspiracy, relationships... Basically anything. It felt good to be part of a group of people who wanted to talk about God all night, however when I decided I was going to do everything in my power to get debt free, the Lord started pulling me away from these groups. The truth was that most of these people talking all night were broke. It's nice to talk about concepts, and I believe in planning and lots of plans, but if you never create a plan and actually execute it, you are wasting time and babbling.

Be honest with yourself, do you babble? I know sometimes I did in the beginning of my marriage, and my husband had to talk to me about it. The more I eliminated this behavior, the more money we made. Or maybe it is a certain friend or significant other that you need to set some boundaries with, as they are wasting your time. Every two or three hours that they talk to you about nothing could be time you are working on your business, ministry, side business, career, etc. Get your time back and set boundaries.

I had to learn to be a little more firm in leaving and walking away from people, or leaving certain gatherings when I felt that conversations were just babbling. People at first might get offended thinking you are being rude or unloving, but your real friends don't see you as their emotional dumping ground. Instead, they will respect your boundaries. This might even be true with family members as well. If a person needs to vent to you for hours each week or each night, they may actually need to spend more time with Jesus, as they are not processing their emotions before the throne but using you as an escape from dealing with the Father. Others may need counseling. Set boundaries and choose debt and poverty freedom over endless talking.

Don't Chase Fantasies

"A hard worker has plenty of food, but a person who chases fantasies ends up in poverty."
Proverbs 28:19 (NLT)

We see from this verse that chasing fantasies can lead to poverty, but what does "chasing fantasies" mean? This can mean many things. One of them can be "get rich quick" schemes or working in lanes that are not yours. It is important to consult God about what your line of work is in this life, so He can prosper you there. It is easy to see other people's flashy lanes and want to be in them, but this can lead to poverty.

When I was younger, I had this revelation about the common phrase, "The grass is always greener on the other side." I once tried to date two guys around the same time, thinking the grass was greener with one than the other. When I went to the new one, I realized it wasn't right, so I tried going back to the old one and he wouldn't take me back. So then I tried to go back to the new one, and he also wouldn't take me back. I ended up with neither of them. This was my revelation; when you leave one grass for a new one, it becomes brown, as you are not watering it and taking care of it. When you go back to it and notice it is brown, you may try to run back to the new grass, but when you get there you realize that one is now also brown, as you had not been watering it. We must stick with the Lord's plan for our lives and not chase fantasies. This is also true with money as you can't just jump on anything that comes your way. It could be a waste of time and lead to poverty when you could have been working your lane. Know the Lord's plan for your finances and stick to that.

If you are not called to a multi-level marketing company (MLM), don't join one. I think some people may be called there, but it's not everyone. These MLM's often show you the millionaires who worked their process, when the average person in the company makes less than $1000 a month, which is not enough to even pay most rents. If you are reading this outside of the US that may seem like a lot, but it's not for Americans. If the Lord tells you to join one of these, then He will bless it, but don't join one unless the Lord says to. If He does tell you to do so, ask Him for His strategies. He may show you different ways or methods than others.

Also be careful of investing in things you know nothing about, unless you have a very trusted advisor you've been working with for years. The stock market can tell you something is "the next big thing", but listen to the prompting of the Holy Spirit on where to invest, as He will show you what lane is for you rather than a get rich quick fantasy. Often if it is too good to be true, it probably is. There are exceptions that the Lord can show you, but ultimately the Lord should be your financial planner. Even if you see a financial planner for advice, go home and pray about the decisions yourself.

Another fantasy that can lead people to poverty is masturbation. I know some of you think this is something you have to do or you can't help as it's "natural", but it is not. That is a lie from the pit of hell, and men and women are secretly doing this by the multitudes, and it is keeping them poor. I am not going to go deep into this as I do not want to cause anyone to stumble, but when I stopped masturbating for a whole year my income quadrupled the next year. Yes, times 4! I never did it again. When you are masturbating you are having sex with someone who never agreed to have sex with you. That is rape. But on a deeper spiritual level, the vision you are seeing in your mind is actually being projected by a demon, and you are having sex with that demon. Then that demon can have access into your life as you have a soul tie with it, and it can steal your money.

Yes, I know some of you are shocked I am talking about sex in a financial book, but I have to tell you the truth. If I just gave you the normal fluff that is traditional 'financial wisdom', you would not get set free. If you don't believe me, try going without masturbation and see what God does with your finances. It will be hard at first because you are used to this demon, but in time as you resist the devil he will flee (James 4:7).

Be Disciplined

"Poverty and shame will come to one who neglects discipline..."
Proverbs 13:18 (NASB)

This is pretty self explanatory, but being a disciplined person will produce wealth, whereas a lack of discipline can create poverty. Say for example you are in sales; It takes discipline to make your sales calls every day. If you start neglecting those calls your income might also go down, as you are now lowering your chances of making sales by not putting in the effort. Though discipline is hard for a time, the reward of discipline is greater. Try not to have an attitude of "I hope God blesses me with wealth one day". Rather, have an attitude of "I can create wealth through the power God has given me." And then go out there and get your prosperity. It takes work and discipline to become wealthy. I have had to do things I don't always want to do. I've spent long hours and late nights working on a product, but when you see the sales coming in and can pay off a debt or pay your kids college tuition… It is worth it. Be disciplined; not so rigid that you never enjoy yourself, but be consistent in creating wealth and paying off debt and you will see fruit.

"And you shall remember the LORD your God, for it is
He who gives you power to get (create) wealth…"
Deuteronomy 8:18 (NKJV)

Be A Hard Worker

"A slack hand causes poverty, but the hand
of the diligent makes rich."
Proverbs 10:4 (ESV)

This is pretty obvious, but people that don't work or are continuously lazy will be poor. You can pray and fast and cry, but if you are not willing to work, you probably won't be rich.

God doesn't reward laziness.

He rewards those who are out there working for Him. The harvest is plentiful, but the laborers are few (Matthew 9:37). If you knew how many hours I work every day on the ministry, you would be shocked. Right now as I am writing this I am pregnant, so it is less than normal, but for many years I worked 10-14 hour days every day. I wouldn't change this, as I am now poverty free, debt free, and have helped thousands of people all over the world know the Word of God in 60 different nations. But I get it, sometimes it is hard to work, sometimes you want to be lazy. And sometimes I think you should take a break; whether it be taking a Sabbath day, going on a vacation, watching your favorite show, going out to the beach, whatever, we all need to recharge so we don't burn out. But be honest with yourself, are you lazy? Are you really working? Let the Holy Spirit speak to you.

Take Time To Make Decisions

"The plans of the diligent lead surely to plenty, But those
of everyone who is hasty, surely to poverty."
Proverbs 21:5 (NKJV)

Do you know people (or maybe you are that person) that seem to live life by the seat of their pants? One minute they are going to take this job, the next they are moving out of the country, the next they are starting a business, the next they are going into ministry… They go wherever they feel in the moment. These people are often not wealthy as they are unstable.

If you really want to be wealthy, get out of debt and break poverty, you must sit still, think, reflect and listen to the Holy Spirit. Running from place to place and making decisions too quickly can make you poor, as you are not fully thinking and hearing God about the situation, rather you are just reacting. I do think sometimes you have to make a decision quickly, but even five minutes with the Lord can help you make the right decision. Do you feel a peace arise about this decision? Or do you feel a lack of peace? If you only have a few minutes to make a decision, trust your peace. But if you have more time, take the time. Think about what the benefits and negatives are of the situation and try to get a Bible verse from the Lord to back up what you are feeling, as well as His rhema. This will keep you safe. The Lord has plans for you, but you will only know them if you sit still and listen.

When You Oppress The Poor You Become Poor

"One who oppresses the poor to make more for himself,
or gives to the rich, will only come to poverty."
Proverbs 22:16 (NASB)

I am hoping none of you are doing this, but when you oppress the poor, poverty may come. Sometimes I see ministers do this as they have everyone volunteering and working for free while they take all the wealth of the church. This is wrong, as a man deserves to be paid for his labor (1 Timothy 5:18). Now, I understand when you are first getting started in ministry you may not make a lot; I didn't, but you can do something. I at least tried to feed my staff when I had no money to pay them, or I gave them goods from my home. I will never forget a house meeting we did in the early years where three members of my team and I shared two packets of ramen noodles. We were so broke, but I shared my ramen with them. I didn't eat a whole packet of ramen and say "good luck" to my team. I'd rather have half a pack of ramen and be in the will of the Lord than eat the whole thing and be out of His will. But God has blessed us immensely for giving and sharing what we had, even though we didn't have a lot.

It may be hard to give when you don't have a lot, but don't use people and give nothing back when money comes in. I would give my workers bags, suitcases, earrings, jewelry, and clothes from my own closet until I could pay them. Do something, bless your workers somehow. God will honor you for this and give you proper money to pay people. And please pay them above the minimum wage as much as you can. People need to eat and feed their families. Don't use people that are hungry for God as slaves. We are all valuable in the kingdom of God, and a man deserves his wages.

Keep Diligent Accounts

"Be thou diligent to know the state of thy flocks,
and look well to thy herds."
Proverbs 27:23 (KJV)

Though this verse does not say that bad accounting directly causes poverty, I believe if you give me liberty, I can explain how it does. In the above verse Solomon tells us to know the state of our flocks and to look well to our herds. For many (except farmers and maybe pastors) this seems unrelatable at first. But when you really pray and reflect on this verse, God is telling you to know what is going on with what you have. Back then, a person's wealth wasn't always in a tangible currency, but rather in the things they had (grains, flocks, fields, etc). It is important to know the state of your finances.

I think there is a temptation when your finances are undesirable to avoid them and let bills pile up, pretending they are not there. But doing this will only make things worse. By not tracking my transactions to a cent, I would often overestimate what I had, leaving me in the negative too often. We must track everything as much as possible. This will often help against fraud as well, because almost daily I check my accounts. I was able to detect fraudulent activity on my personal account three different times while the charges were still pending, so they never actually affected my account. The bankers when I came in were shocked that I would notice something so quickly, as most people would have taken longer. But it is because I am diligent to know the state of my flocks and herds that I saw the fraud and the banks were able to dispute and cancel the charges. How much of what we go through financially is because we are not thorough?

The first thing you need to track is your monthly expenses (rent, mortgage, electric, phone, car, etc). Then your annual expenses. Then your fluctuating monthly spending, such as the average you spend on groceries each month, the average you spend on gas, the average you spend on entertainment, the average you spend on eating out, etc. The best way to do this is to track four months and then come up with an average. It is unlikely any month will be exactly the same, but by finding the average you will be able to put that in your monthly expenses as a "bill". Even if you are off a little bit you will know the average, and this will give you a good idea of whether you are overspending or of the income you need to bring in each month to cover everything.

I think another thing you should do is cushion this amount. If you only give yourself the exact amount of bills and fluctuating spending you will often error. You need a cushion of at least $100 for an extra meal, extra clothing for a wedding, extra gift to buy, etc. Things will come up, without a cushion you will always feel strapped. Some months you won't spend the cushion and some months you will, but you need a little extra to help you live the life you want to live.

Some bills can be prayed through, but you have to see them and acknowledge them to pray through them. The truth sets free. You also have to not blame companies for bills they send you that you agreed to. This victim mentality will keep you stuck. Instead, repent to the Lord for buying something or doing something you can't afford, and ask Him for steps to pay it. Don't put your head in the sand. Conqueror your finances with Christ.

Another financial tip is knowing the dates that things are due. I see people pay way too much money in late fees, when late fees can be avoided by simply knowing what is going on. This is a waste of money and could be used to further the kingdom or just feed your family. So try to make sure you have a place you see often where you can easily visualize all the due dates of your bills.

Don't Be Stingy

"One gives freely, yet grows all the richer; another withholds what he should give, and only suffers want."
Proverbs 11:24 (BSB)

This is an interesting dynamic in scripture on the surface and mathematically, but it says when you withhold what you should give you become poor. How can you keep your money and then become poor? Well, it is because of the way God's kingdom works. The next verse in scripture says that the generous person will prosper (Proverbs 11:25). We are in a kingdom of sowing and reaping. If we sow, we reap. When we give money, we receive money.

Now the question remains, how do you know what you "should" give? In other words, how much should you give and when and where should you do it? I believe quite simply it is listening to the Holy Spirit inside of you. I believe in tithing. I know some Christians don't, but I think this is the beginning of giving. We should try to do more than just give to the church, but also to non-traditional ministries and individuals as the Lord would lead you. It could be items, cash, or time. But listen to the promptings of giving. Do not be afraid to give. There was a week in church when Ryan and I were so broke that all we had to give was change that we found on the ground. Because we were so broke, I would collect every penny, nickel or dime I found on the ground and use it towards groceries. Yes, it was that bad in the beginning. Yes, I was still serving the Lord and in ministry in those seasons. Normally that change was food money, but at church one Sunday I just put all the change I had found in the offering, because I trusted God. I now have no debt and can buy whatever food I want whenever I want to, but I gave when He prompted.

Giving is love. We love God, His church, His people, His ministries, and so we give into these things. The Bible says love never fails (1 Corinthians 13:8). So if you sow love, you will not fail. I am not telling you to give everything you have all the time, though I think sometimes God calls for that. But I am telling you to give when He prompts. When we don't, we are not trusting God. The more you do this, the more you learn to trust Him. The harvest could be quick, or it may take time, but it will come.

Now that you have an understanding of ways that the Bible says can cause poverty, my prayer is that you do not give into these things, but rather apply these principles to your life and break poverty.

Lord I pray that the person reading this will apply these principles to their life and will be free of poverty in Jesus's name amen.

I also believe poverty is a spirit, a spirit that tells you to give into the above such as laziness, stinginess, hastiness, overeating, overdrinking, etc. When you are tempted to do any of these things, rebuke the spirit of poverty in your life and choose wealth and freedom instead. Wealth is a choice. You must understand that. Many people choose to be poor by giving into these and other things. We have to have discipline and choose abundance.

Part 3

New Covenant Promise

Another way to choose into abundance is the presence of God. Under the new covenant, we experience blessings not just from principles but also from being with Jesus. I want you to think about the story of when the multitudes followed Jesus for three days with no food. These people weren't working, but rather just being with Jesus. Jesus tells the disciples to feed the people as they had been with Him days without food, and they may collapse:

> *"I feel sorry for these people. They have been here with*
> *me for three days, and they have nothing left to eat. If I*
> *send them home hungry, they will faint along the way.*
> *For some of them have come a long distance."*
> *Mark 8:2-3 (NLT)*

There have been times in my walk with God that I have barely had any food to eat and didn't know where my next meal was coming from, but if you have been with Jesus in the way He wants you to, He will provide. In our study of Proverbs in the previous section, I mentioned that a slack hand can lead to poverty (Proverbs 10:4). However, these people experienced overflow despite the fact that they were not working because they were with Jesus.

This is why it is important to know when you are being lazy and it is causing poverty versus when you are spending time with Jesus. This is a fine line. Some people work so much and are still broke, because they work in the flesh not doing what work the Lord wants them to do. Are you in the God anointed lane for you? Others pretend they are spending time with Jesus so they don't have to work, and then blame their problems on others and the government when they just need to get to work. God says to take care of the poor, not the lazy. However, being in His presence is not lazy. God will kick me out of my alone time with

Him when I need to get to work. If we are only alone in the presence, we are only helping ourselves. We must fill up and then pour out and do it again. There is balance, but if He called you to three days alone with Him, that is not lazy. That is obedience. The multitudes were about to be rewarded for just spending time with God:

"And He instructed the crowd to sit down on the ground. Then He took the seven loaves, gave thanks and broke them, and gave them to His disciples to set before the people. And they distributed them to the crowd. They also had a few small fish, and Jesus blessed them and ordered that these be set before them as well. The people ate and were satisfied, and the disciples picked up seven basketfuls of broken pieces that were left over."

Mark 8:6-8 (BSB)

They went from nothing to more than enough just from being with Jesus. Sometimes we need to obey Proverbs to get wealth, and sometimes we just need to be with Jesus. Remember that Jesus's wisdom is above Solomon's wisdom:

*"The Queen of the South will rise at the judgment
With this generation and condemn it; for she came from
the ends of the earth to hear the wisdom of Solomon,
and now One greater than Solomon is here."*
Matthew 12:42 (BSB)

What Jesus says supersedes what Solomon says. Solomon's wisdom is a good foundation for wealth and success, but the Holy Spirit knows more.

Part 4

Your Debt Freedom

Now let's get down to business. It is time to get you out of debt. This will be the part of the book where you interact with your story, your finances, and your spirituality in order to be free from the feeling of bondage that is debt. Take a minute to breathe. **You can be poverty and debt free.** Remember the blood of Jesus, that is enough. No matter what contracts you signed, or what bills have piled up, or if other people's bills have fallen in your lap. The Bible says where the Spirit of the Lord is there is freedom (2 Corinthians 3:17). You can be free; His Spirit will guide you.

That I believe is the power of this book compared with others, the Holy Spirit and Jesus. You can get out of debt, but if you don't break poverty, you can get back into it again. Also, The Holy Spirit will make this an individual and unique experience of freedom, as you are different from everyone else. There is no formula to get out of debt and poverty, it is a person. That Person is Jesus, and He will be with you every step of the way. Whether this process takes moments, months or even years, the Lord will hold your hand and guide you step by step if you are open to listening to Him and engage in the process. It is time to be free.

Father God, I pray you help bring freedom to people from debt as they engage with you in the process. May you show them the truths and unlock the doors they need you to.

First let's make a list of all your debts. Put exact numbers here:

	Name of Debt	Amount Owed
1		
2		
3		
4		
5		
6		
7		
8		
9		
10		
11		
Total Amount Owed:		

Next, let's take a second and repent for any of those debts you got into that God didn't want you in. Some may be inherited or something else, but let the Lord reveal the ones you got into out of sin. Also, let's see if you are angry at any of these debt collectors. You must forgive them.

The Bible says:

> *"And forgive us our debts, as we also forgive our debtors."*
> *Matthew 6:12 (GNV)*

But as you go on in the chapter, it also says,

> *"For if ye do forgive men their trespasses,*
> *your heavenly Father will also forgive you.*
> *Matthew 6:14 (GNV)*

This is a key to debt forgiveness; forgiving your debtor and letting go of the anger. Most of the time you signed this debt willingly, often not reading the fine print. You must take responsibility for that, even if they treated you unfairly. You must still forgive them in your heart, and the Lord will forgive you of the debt. When He does, things will change.

Now let's go through each of these debts with the Lord and see if there are any principalities or heart issues with you or with the organization that need to be healed or broken. For example, there could be a car dealership that has a spirit of python over it that is trying to stop you from getting free, and you need to be aware of that and break it in Jesus' name. Keep praying over the principality until you feel peace to stop praying. Remember my story and how when I broke the principality over my car loan, things started changing. Some fights are spiritual.

Other times it is your heart that is stopping you or maybe theirs. Maybe their pride is stopping them from setting you free, as they like to lord over people. Or maybe you like to be the victim or are used to be the victim, and you really need to step into being the conqueror Christ called you to be.

List what the Lord tells you for each debt on the next page:

	Heart Issues or Principalities
Debt 1	
Debt 2	
Debt 3	
Debt 4	
Debt 5	
Debt 6	
Debt 7	
Debt 8	
Debt 9	
Debt 10	
Debt 11	

Now the next question is where to begin? Starting can be overwhelming. Take a minute and ask the Lord which debt you should conqueror with Him first. If you are not sure what He is saying, sometimes the smallest one is easiest and can give you a feeling of victory and motivation to get the next one. Some people feel led to start with the one that has the highest interest rate. Whatever you feel peace about is fine.

Once you know where to start, the next question might be, "But how do I do it?" There is no cookie cutter answer here, but here are some suggestions:

1. You can sell stuff on Craigslist, eBay, a garage sale, luxury resale websites, etc.

2. You can lower your bills by taking time to research other companies that do the same thing. For example, a cell phone company can give you similar service for a cheaper price, or the same with car insurance. Shop around and find the best deals for you.

3. You can find ways to make more money such as getting a part time job somewhere, starting a small business, or babysitting kids in the neighborhood, etc.

4. You can start couponing and saving on your groceries, gas or date nights, and take that money to pay off debt.

Does this area spark any ideas from the Lord? Things to sell? Bills to lower? Write them here:

_____

_____

_____

_____

_____

_____

_____

_____

Now it's time to create an action plan for your debt. Ask the Lord what He wants you to do for each of your debts specifically. Remember, God told Noah how to build the ark detail by detail. He may give you the entire plan at once, or He may just give you step one. That first small step may not pay off the full debt; you may have to go back to Him to get step two or three or four.

Debt 1 Action Plan from God: What did He say to do?

_____

_____

_____

_____

_____

_____

_____

_____

Debt 1 Step Checklist: If God gave you specific steps, list them here and check them off as you complete them.

☐ _____

☐ _____

☐ _____

☐ _____

☐ _____

☐ _____

☐ _____

☐ _____

☐ _____

☐ _____

☐ _____

☐ _____

☐ _____

☐ _____

☐ I completed this plan   ☐ God paid off this debt!

Debt 2 Action Plan from God: What did He say to do?

_____

_____

_____

_____

_____

_____

_____

_____

Debt 2 Step Checklist: If God gave you specific steps, list them here and check them off as you complete them.

☐ _____

☐ _____

☐ _____

☐ _____

☐ _____

☐ _____

☐ _____

☐ _____

☐ _____

☐ _____

☐ _____

☐ _____

☐ _____

☐ _____

☐ I completed this plan   ☐ God paid off this debt!

Debt 3 Action Plan from God: What did He say to do?

_____

_____

_____

_____

_____

_____

_____

_____

Debt 3 Step Checklist: If God gave you specific steps, list them here and check them off as you complete them.

☐ _____

☐ _____

☐ _____

☐ _____

☐ _____

☐ _____

☐ _____

☐ _____

☐ _____

☐ _____

☐ _____

☐ _____

☐ _____

☐ _____

☐ I completed this plan   ☐ God paid off this debt!

Debt 4 Action Plan from God: What did He say to do?

_____

_____

_____

_____

_____

_____

_____

_____

Debt 4 Step Checklist: If God gave you specific steps, list them here and check them off as you complete them.

☐ _____

☐ _____

☐ _____

☐ _____

☐ _____

☐ _____

☐ _____

☐ _____

☐ _____

☐ _____

☐ _____

☐ _____

☐ _____

☐ _____

☐ _____

☐ I completed this plan   ☐ God paid off this debt!

Debt 5 Action Plan from God: What did He say to do?

_____

_____

_____

_____

_____

_____

_____

_____

Debt 5 Step Checklist: If God gave you specific steps, list them here and check them off as you complete them.

☐ _____

☐ _____

☐ _____

☐ _____

☐ _____

☐ _____

☐ _____

☐ _____

☐ _____

☐ _____

☐ _____

☐ _____

☐ _____

☐ _____

☐ I completed this plan   ☐ God paid off this debt!

Debt 6 Action Plan from God: What did He say to do?

_____

_____

_____

_____

_____

_____

_____

_____

Debt 6 Step Checklist: If God gave you specific steps, list them here and check them off as you complete them.

☐ _____

☐ _____

☐ _____

☐ _____

☐ _____

☐ _____

☐ _____

☐ _____

☐ _____

☐ _____

☐ _____

☐ _____

☐ _____

☐ _____

☐ _____

☐ I completed this plan   ☐ God paid off this debt!

Debt 7 Action Plan from God: What did He say to do?

_____

_____

_____

_____

_____

_____

_____

_____

Debt 7 Step Checklist: If God gave you specific steps, list them here and check them off as you complete them.

☐ _____

☐ _____

☐ _____

☐ _____

☐ _____

☐ _____

☐ _____

☐ _____

☐ _____

☐ _____

☐ _____

☐ _____

☐ _____

☐ _____

☐ I completed this plan   ☐ God paid off this debt!

Debt 8 Action Plan from God: What did He say to do?

_____

_____

_____

_____

_____

_____

_____

_____

Debt 8 Step Checklist: If God gave you specific steps, list them here and check them off as you complete them.

☐ _____

☐ _____

☐ _____

☐ _____

☐ _____

☐ _____

☐ _____

☐ _____

☐ _____

☐ _____

☐ _____

☐ _____

☐ _____

☐ _____

☐ I completed this plan   ☐ God paid off this debt!

Debt 9 Action Plan from God: What did He say to do?

_____

_____

_____

_____

_____

_____

_____

_____

Debt 9 Step Checklist: If God gave you specific steps, list them here and check them off as you complete them.

☐ _____

☐ _____

☐ _____

☐ _____

☐ _____

☐ _____

☐ _____

☐ _____

☐ _____

☐ _____

☐ _____

☐ _____

☐ _____

☐ _____

☐ I completed this plan   ☐ God paid off this debt!

Debt 10 Action Plan from God: What did He say to do?

_____

_____

_____

_____

_____

_____

_____

Debt 10 Step Checklist: If God gave you specific steps, list them here and check them off as you complete them.

☐ _____

☐ _____

☐ _____

☐ _____

☐ _____

☐ _____

☐ _____

☐ _____

☐ _____

☐ _____

☐ _____

☐ _____

☐ _____

☐ _____

☐ I completed this plan   ☐ God paid off this debt!

Debt 11 Action Plan from God: What did He say to do?

_____

_____

_____

_____

_____

_____

_____

_____

Debt 11 Step Checklist: If God gave you specific steps, list them here and check them off as you complete them.

☐ _____

☐ _____

☐ _____

☐ _____

☐ _____

☐ _____

☐ _____

☐ _____

☐ _____

☐ _____

☐ _____

☐ _____

☐ _____

☐ _____

☐ I completed this plan   ☐ God paid off this debt!

The plan from God could be difficult or time consuming, but trust the process. He may give you a different plan for each debt. There could be different principalities with each debt, so don't get into formulas unless He says to do them all the same. Check them off as you go and pray through it. Pray over the debt until it is gone. Remember, every dollar counts. Even $10 towards the debt makes it go down. Little by little it will go away, and sometimes a large chunk or favor can knock it out. Be nice to debt collectors, they are people. But say what the Lord would tell you and when for ultimate favor. You got this.

I also wanted to attach to this book an example of a monthly budget (located on the next page) for you to copy so you can stay on top of things, and so when you do get out of debt you don't get back in. Remember the sting you felt being in it. Don't go back quickly. You may have to delay gratification at times, but it will be worth it for the sake of being free. When I got free of debt, I felt like a weight just lifted off me. A weight that I carried for years. My mind was free from thinking about money so often, and I was able to do more for the kingdom as my mind was more free.

Sample Monthly Budget Sheet:

Bill	Amount	Due Date
Mortgage/Rent		
Electric Bill		
Cell Phone		
Car Payment		
Monthly Subscriptions		
Average Groceries		
Average Gas		
Average Entertainment		
Average Eating Out/Date Nights		
Average Beauty/Health		
Gym Membership		
Minimum Debt Payment(s)		
Other		
Total Bills		

Total Amount of Current Income: _____

If you see that your bills are more than your current income, it is time to ask the Lord how to make more money. It could be selling stuff, a second job, rental property, getting a higher paying job, etc. If the amount is under, you may still need to make money in order to put more money towards the debt.

If you do have some extra cash, ask the Lord how much to put towards what debt each month. Try to focus on one at a time to create momentum, unless He really tells you otherwise.

Conclusion

It is possible to be debt and poverty free, if you do the work, apply certain principles to your life, and pray against these demons that want to keep you stuck. You got this. The Holy Spirit lives inside of you and will guide you every step of the way. Keep this book in your sight until you are out of debt so you are motivated to mark off another debt on the list. When you get out of a debt, do something for yourself, even a small reward to breathe and motivate yourself for the next one (only if He says of course). You really can live a different life. I have done it, and I am not different from you. I just had discipline, prayed, applied God's word to my life, and followed the direction of the Holy Spirit. You can do it too.